Thank you for purchas.  .jok:

Bow Drill Trou..ie Shooting:

Case Studies in Friction Fire Lighting

I hope you enjoy it and would welcome any comments or
reviews, if you would like to get in touch with me via social
media or my blog to let me know what you think you will be
entitled to a free full colour download of the kindle version of
this book

If you are interested in the original piece of research that this
book is based on it can be found on my Academia page at;

https://reaseheath.academia.edu/GeoffreyGuy

Thanks for reading

Bow Drill Trouble Shooting:

Case Studies in Friction Fire Lighting

By Geoffrey Guy

Dedication

For My Sallie, Michael and Lillie and my Mum and Dad who have all had to put up with sticks, wood shavings, animal skins and funny smells.

Acknowledgements

Thanks to all those who made this project possible;

To the Extended Diploma Countryside Management Students from Moulton College (class of 2013-14) pictured below. Thank you for taking part in this project and giving it your best, even if you did turn some of the feedback sessions into bushcraft innuendo competitions!

Thanks to Graham Harvey, Senior Lecturer at Trinity St David Carmarthen for your feedback and support with this project which I wrote up as part of my Masters studies in Outdoor Education.

Thanks to Richard Guy for his photographic expertise and to him and Sallie Guy for taking all the pictures for this book. Also to Joseph Guy for kindly whittling some of the drills and hearths featured in this book.

Finally Thanks to Hyrum Jolliffe and Dad (Martin Guy) for beautifully modelling a team bow drill (even though only Dad's foot made it into the final edit).

Contents

Introduction 1

The Basics of the Bow Drill.................................7

Case Studies 13

Material 15

Wrong Wood (Species) 16

I Can't Find A Curved Stick for A Bow 22

Wood Crumbles/Deforms Without Producing An Ember..........23

Notch Too Small/Wide..25

Wet Wood...27

String Tension 29

Wrong Diameter 30

Drill Too Large (Diameter)...33

Drill Deformities...35

The Drill Gets Shiny 39

'Smoking Hand'..41

The Hearth Board Is Too Thick.....................................44

The Bow Is Bending When I Try To Drill......................................45

Method and Technique 47

More Pressure...48

I Can't Hold The Drill Steady 51

Use The Whole Bow..53

The Drill Keeps Slipping Off The Hearth..............................54

Managing Your Ember and Lighting a Fire 55

I Have Made An Ember I Think?...56

The Ember Falls Apart When I Put It In The Tinder Bundle 58

The Ember Grows At First But Then Goes Out...........................64

I Get Smoke In My Eyes..65

I Made Fire!! Now what? 66

Activities for teaching the bow drill..........................67

Learning Logs; 68

Peer Teaching..69

Recording comments 70

'Speed dating' 71

Socratic questioning..72

Team Activities..73

Conclusion..75

References 81

BushcraftEducation 83

Introduction

Between October and December 2013 I carried out a project with students to help develop their skills in bow drill fire lighting.

They were studying towards an extended diploma in countryside management and due to the needs of the industry they were preparing to enter and a particular interest from the students a module on adventurous activities was added to their course to prepare them to lead groups outdoors as they might be expected to do in their future careers. Bushcraft, particularly bow drill fire lighting, was one of the activities delivered as part of this module. My write up of this project was submitted in partial fulfilment of the requirements of a Master's Degree in Outdoor Education and its rationale was partly to help me make improvements to the way I teach friction fire lighting. I hoped that encouraging students to reflect on their performance and technique without intensive instruction and tuition might help them internalise and remember what they learned. I hoped that this would improve students practical ability by developing their underpinning knowledge of friction fire lighting, not theoretical knowledge in terms of the science of the topic but the 'knowledge in action' (Schon, 1987), the knowledge which relates directly to the execution of the task. In terms of friction fire lighting this knowledge might include a knowledge of the properties of different woody plant and tree species, where to find them, which are best for the task, a knowledge of the best position to use, how to address problems and obstacles such as 'smoking hand' (see page 53). Having this knowledge or developing it through reflection would allow them to consistently light a fire. This consistency or retention of knowledge and the ability to apply it characterises 'deep learning', a superficial or surface knowledge of a topic which will only allow the acceptance and memorization of facts (Houghton, 2004) does not equip students with the skills and knowledge they will require to retain, replicate or apply knowledge.

My reason for looking at ways of encouraging students to develop their skills through their own reflection rather than my intervention was that when I learned practical bushcraft skills I did so without the direction of an instructor or tutor in an 'unmediated' (Laurillard , 1993) fashion, I learned mostly from my own reflection and experience and from some material I gleaned from books. I am convinced that, although my skills may have developed slower without someone to facilitate the improvement of my technique, I am now well equipped to facilitate learning in others because I have experienced the same mistakes that they have, I can spot the inefficiencies in their technique or suggest a different approach to try because I learned by reflecting on my mistakes when those same changes were necessary. It is this conviction that first led me to consider looking at the value of reflection with my students.

I chose to try and facilitate reflection and deeper learning by using learning logs. Each student would complete a brief workbook which would help them record the outcome of each attempt with the bow drill, what they had changed during their attempt and whether they thought they needed to make further changes before the next attempt. I chose to use learning logs for a number of reasons, partly because of my experience of using a diary to record my own progress as I continue to develop bushcraft skills, partly because of earlier success I have had using similar logs, journals and portfolios with students, and partly due to the potential benefit of notes as an 'aide-mémoire' (Petty, 2004), and of the benefit of the note taking process on the students ability to learn and retain information (Piolat, et al., 2005). I also hoped that these logs would encourage "involvement and ownership of learning" (Moon , 2006) and force the student into an active role (Jensen, 1987), not just engaging with the practical task at hand but an engagement with learning **from** the activity and trying to learn how to improve rather than just 'having a go'. As well as engaging the students I wanted to promote understanding and long term retention of concepts, not just facts, facilitating future application of skills and knowledge (Houghton, 2004). This is what I wanted to facilitate, not just the skills to make fire once but the knowledge and understanding of the entire process which would allow students to make fire again and again even without my 'mediation'.

In some respects this project ended in failure as the students failed to engage with the learning logs as I had hoped, several of them didn't complete them at all and most of those who did didn't really use them to reflect on their performance or suggest improvements but rather superficially described what they had done. Perhaps I should have expected this, after all why would they want to write something when they could do something practical?

Although there was no consistent engagement with the learning logs students found other ways to reflect on their progress. One of the most effective alternatives to the learning log was when the students started recording observations they made about their project on a whiteboard, The first comment that went up was "I used a spoon knife instead" by a students who had struggled to make a depression in the bearing block with the point of a knife and who used a crook knife instead. From there the whiteboard was soon filled with comments, obstacles and solutions.

Prompted by their comments and insight into the problems, and obstacles they faced as they learned to light a fire with a bow drill I have prepared a list of case studies on a range of common problems encountered when learning to bow drill and how to overcome them.

The Basics of the
Bow Drill

The bow drill is the first method of friction fire lighting that many learn, it offers considerable advantages over any other method as it requires no specialist tools to construct, no complicated components need to be fabricated and the use of a bow drastically increases our capacity to rotate a drill under pressure compared, for example, with trying to use the hand drill method where the rotation and downward pressure must all be applied to the drill with your hands.

All the components of a bow drill fire kit are shown in this picture;

Bow – this should not be flexible, no longer than your arm and preferably no shorter than you forearm. This will probably have to be made from green wood to make sure it strong enough to put up with constant use.

String – synthetic cord such as nylon para-cord is ideal.

Drill - one end should be blunt to maximize friction the other pointed to minimize it, the one pictured above is made of aspen.

Hearth – this can be made from the same piece of wood as the drill although this is not essential, the one pictured above is made of aspen. The wood for both hearth and drill will need to be made from dead dry wood and can be whittled from a single piece or separate pieces depending on what you can find but there is no need for one piece to be softer or harder than the other.

Ember Catcher – this can be as simple as a dry leaf or piece of bark or purpose made from wood as pictured above. Its purpose is to catch the ember as it forms and stop it touching the cold/damp ground and also to allow you to easily move the ember to your tinder.

Bearing Block – Something to apply pressure to the drill, it can be made of wood, bone, stone or anything else that provides you with a good grip and which won't create too much friction against the drill, the one pictured above is made of dogwood.

Once you have all the pieces of your bow drill kit dig a small notch in the hearth piece with the point of your knife, place the point of the drill in the notch and drill gently until a depression has been formed and both the

wood of the hearth and the drill tip has become slightly charred as in the example of a willow drill and hearth 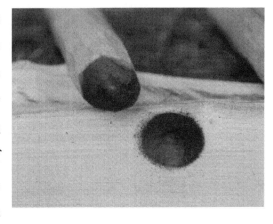 above. Now you can cut a v shaped notch (the hearth in the picture to the left is made of elm) out of the hearth from the center of the depression to the edge and place the ember pan under the notch. Start drilling again until a continuous stream of smoke comes from the pile of black shavings which will accumulate in the notch. Once you are satisfied that you have created an ember stop drilling and carefully lift the drill away from the hearth, don't just let the drill spin away as it might break up the

 ember. Use a twig or the tip of your knife to push all the black powder which will become the 'coal' that you will use to light your tinder together as you move the hearth out of the way. You can blow very gently on the coal or fan it with your hand to provide a bit of extra air and help it grow. You will see it start to glow before long and now you can carefully transfer it to your tinder bundle, make sure you don't tip it in from a great height as it will break up and go out. From this point on you will need to blow it into life just as with any other fire, except remember that the coal is very fragile and will need some coaxing and care.

Case Studies

The case studies and tips which follow are based on my experience of bow drill fire lighting and the project I carried out with students, they are split into three sections;

Materials; selection of material and fabrication of bow drill fire lighting kit.

Method and Technique; your position, how to apply the necessary pressure, techniques for fire lighting as a team etc...

Managing your Ember and Lighting a Fire; the final stage of the process, now that you have created an ember how are you going to light your fire?

Material

From left to right; Willow, Aspen, Clematis, Elder, Ivy

Wrong Wood (Species)

A lot of the case studies which follow will talk about the right/wrong wood based on its properties but first consider the species of wood you choose. Knowing what properties to look for in a piece of wood when selecting material for friction fire lighting is going to be a key skill and will help you be able to identify useful resources even when you may not be familiar with the species in a particular area but it is important to know a few species to begin with.

This table describes my experience of some common UK tree's and woody shrubs, they have been categorised A- for my first choice, the best woods for fire lighting, B- for second choices, woods which are still very successful but not quite as easy to work with, C- last resort woods which I have used successfully but which are not easy to work with, or X woods which are not useful for the hearth and drill of a bow drill friction fire set.

Species		Notes
Alder	**B**	A water loving species which when dead and dry can produce very good hearth's and drills.
Aspen	**B**	Not common in the South of the UK but sometimes found if it has been planted, the dead wood goes soft quite quickly so it may be hard to find hard enough wood for drills and hearths.
Birch	**C**	Chars well but seems quite inconsistent when it comes to actually producing an ember.
Blackthorn	**X**	Very hard, polishes quickly and produces little friction.
Clematis	**A**	An excellent choice but difficult to find in useful sizes, sometimes a drill must be put together out of a

		longer straighter piece of wood and fitted with a clematis tip. It is quite a hard wood and very fibrous, perhaps this is why it seems to work so well, maybe the fibrous nature produces that much more friction? Whatever the difficulty in processing clematis and making it ready to use is well worth it.
Elder	**A**	Readily available in lowland areas, elder is relatively short lived and plenty of dead standing shrubs can be found which provide ample material for fire lighting. The long strait shoots however are rarely useful as the centre of the shoot is often made up of a large percentage of soft pith which can mean they collapse easily, you may have to put in a bit of effort whittling a drill and/or hearth from a larger, sounder piece of wood. Elder is in my opinion the best **readily available**

		wood for friction fire lighting in the UK.
Elm	**A**	Not all that easy to find after the ravages of Dutch Elms Disease but where it is available it is an excellent wood for friction fires, it is very fibrous and hard but produces excellent results, perhaps because it is so hard it also seems to spin really easily.
Field Maple	**C**	A very hard wood but can be used successfully to produce embers.
Hazel	**C**	Chars well but seems quite inconsistent when it comes to actually producing an ember.
Hawthorn	**X**	Very dense but not quite as hard as oak or blackthorn, not suitable.
Ivy	**B**	Like Clematis sometimes difficult to find in the appropriate size for hearth's and drill's, the thin vines are not suitable and using a knife to split and baton larger woody pieces

		is very difficult as the grain does not run strait so you might have to do quite a bit of time consuming sawing and whittling to get the pieces you want. The difficulty in processing it is the only reason that I have graded Ivy as a B, otherwise it is excellent.
Lime	**B**	Similar to willow, quite soft and very easy to work with.
Oak	**X**	A very hard wood, always seems to become highly polished under friction and never begins to char.
Sycamore	**C**	Slightly harder than willow or lime but not a bad option.
Willow	**A**	Quite a soft wood and if you can find long strait coppiced willow less whittling may be required than for elder, these stems can be cut green and left to dry, it will dry very fast if the bark is stripped off. Relatively soft wood easy to work with, so

		hearth and drills can be produced quickly from larger timber if necessary. Char's easily but wears out very fast if you are using it with a harder material, for example a willow hearth with an elder drill.

Note: this table addresses the suitability of the species listed purely with regards to their use as drill or hearth, any shown here to be unsuitable could still be used as a bow or bearing block.

I Can't Find A Curved Stick for A Bow

This doesn't have to be a big problem but there is a solution that may seem obvious which definitely won't work: Couldn't you bend a stick and put a bow string on it? Remember that if it's flexible enough to bend it will be so flexible that it will bend rather than spinning the drill. A strait stick can be used almost as effectively as a standard bow with the correct technique;

 Notice that in this picture the drill is on the opposite side of the string to the bow, I would normally have the drill inside the string as the curve of the bow still allows the drill to rotate but with a strait sick the drill will have to be on the opposite side otherwise it will rub against the bow.

Wood Crumbles/Deforms Without Producing An Ember

A common problem at the earliest stage of the fire lighting process is that the wood selected for either the drill or  hearth is too soft and when pressure is applied it crumbles or deforms without producing any heat. The drill tip may become deformed instead of charring as in the picture above or the hearth may wear away without charring like in the picture below. To avoid this you need to be quite selective about the wood you choose, even if you are sure it is a 'good' wood for bow drill fire lighting such as elder or willow not every piece is going to be suitable. Check that the wood is not too soft by pressing it with your thumb nail, if it deforms very easily it will be too soft and will not withstand the

pressure of drilling. Other clues that might indicate the wood will be too soft are lots of woodworm tunnels, or a lot of dust or 'punk' in the piece you are carving your drill and hearth from.

Note: you may find that when using a softer hearth with a harder drill (or vice-versa) that one is used up much quicker than the other; this isn't necessarily a problem as long as it lasts long enough to create an ember but you may find that you need to replace pieces of your kit quite often. For example clematis drills seem to burn through softer hearth boards very quickly.

Notch Too Small/Wide

The notch created in the hearth boards is where the ember will collect and build, without it the charred dust will be flung out of the depression created by the spinning drill and cool down too quickly to be used to create an ember. Compare the picture above of an un-notched hearth board to the picture on the next page of a hearth board with a correctly positioned notch. You will notice that in the notched hearth the charred wood which will become the 'coal' has collected and will be able to form an ember. As a general rule this notch should be approximately an eighth of the drill hole. If it is smaller the ember will not form easily and if it is larger you will find that the drill slips out of the hearth when under pressure and you will struggle to spin it for long enough to create an ember.

Note: it can be tricky to carve a notch with a knife, the wood may be particularly hard or you may just be tired, it is perfectly possible to cut the notch with a saw but just be careful not to over-cut as that will produce a notch that is much too big.

Wet Wood

Without dry wood fire lighting becomes very difficult, even more so when fire lighting by friction. To make sure the components of your kit are dry you may need to prepare them in advance, yes it is possible to start drilling slowly and over a long period of time speed up, resting the drill (and your arms) from time to time and **possibly** produce an ember using green wood but this is very time consuming, tiring and no guarantee of success. If you look at native peoples who relied or still rely on friction as the source of ignition for their fires they always carry with them ready prepared friction fire kit's rather than relying on being able to collect them as they go. Just as you would carry a match or a lighter they carry a friction fire kit and if you want to be consistently successful you need a pre prepared kit as well.

Standing dead wood is the best kind to harvest for any camp fire use and the same goes for bow drill fire lighting, elder is a great resource in this respect as it is relatively short lived and very abundant in lowland areas of the UK so you can always find suitable material. It is also considered to be a weed tree as it limits the growth of other plants underneath it and is a very poor hedgerow plant, it does produce useful berries and flowers but no one is going to complain if you cut a bit of elder for your friction fire set. However even dead standing wood can sometimes have some moisture content and to make fire lighting as easy as possible if you can prepare your hearth and drill a few days/weeks in advance you will give yourself the best chance possible.

To test if the wood is slightly damp you can touch it to your lip, if it feels particularly cold then it may well have some moisture in it.

Note: remember bow drill fire lighting is very tiring and you may not have the energy or strength to drill for a long time, the quicker the fire is lit the less energy you need to use to make it so in terms of a survival situation the quicker you can make fire the better. Also if you make sure your kit is completely dry and prepared in advance you will suffer less disappointments as you practice and study fire lighting

String Tension

The tension of the bow string is quite important, if it's much too loose the drill wont spin at all, if it's a little bit too loose the drill will spin a bit but as you increase downward pressure it will begin to slip and the string will wear out very fast. If the string is too tight any slight wobble as you drill might send it spinning away, possibly cracking you in the knuckles on the way. For a drill about

at thick as your thumb the picture to the left shows roughly the tension you need in the string. You may also find that the string you use stretches slightly as you use it and you may have to tighten it from time to time. It is important that you adjust the string as soon as you realise there is a problem. There is no point trying to force a drill round with a slightly too loose string as you will never produce the necessary friction and you will wear yourself out and break your string.

Wrong Diameter

The ideal diameter for a drill for use with a bow is about the thickness of your thumb, smaller diameter drills won't capitalise on the advantage of having a bow to spin the drill and a bearing block to apply additional pressure. Thinner drills are best for hand drill fire lighting, If you were to use a drill as thick as you do for the bow drill method for hand drilling you would find that the additional friction created by the larger surface area between hearth and drill tip would stop you spinning it with the force required to create enough friction for an ember to form. Although using a drill with a small diameter may still work as it will be easier to spin the thinner drill under pressure than it would be to spin a thicker one you may encounter the following difficulties;

- The smaller contact area between drill and hearth will not capitalise on the advantage in terms of pressure and speed that using a bow and bearing block gives you.
- The increased pressure produced through the use of a bearing block when bow drilling may cause a smaller diameter drill to bend or snap.

- The smaller diameter drill will burn through hearth boards very fast.

- The smaller diameter burn into the hearth board will equate to a smaller notch and therefore less potential to collect a large ember. Compare the picture to the left

with the picture below; the first shows an ember produced from a thumb thickness willow drill on a willow hearth, the picture which follows shows the same hearth and a hazel drill a little thicker than a pencil, using the pound coin for scale can you see the difference in the ember size between the two drills? The larger ember will be much easier to work with

Drill Too Large (Diameter)

A drill much thicker than your thumb will be more difficult to spin using the bow drill method. You need to tread a fine line between maximising friction without making the drill so thick that you can't spin it. Somewhere around the thickness of your thumb seems to be ideal but some variation is acceptable If the drill is too thick the extra friction will not only make it very hard to spin but you will need to apply more pressure the drill will stick causing the string to slip and wear out. Also wider drills become

flattened very quickly producing wide shallow burns into the hearth board, as you have to apply more pressure on the bow to spin the drill what you will often find is that you will push or pull the tip of the drill around creating something I have come to call a 'wandering hole'; The close-up picture on the next page shows how the hole being burnt into the hearth is actually larger than the drill tip. This will reduce the amount of friction in any one place as the drill tip no longer contacts the sides of the burn but just the bottom. This wider burn also allows the charred dust which you want to collect to form an ember to spread out into the sides of the burn and cool down without producing and ember or collecting in the notch. You will also find that as the burn is wider and shallower the drill will more easily slip out leading to another painful crack on the knuckles as it disappears into the undergrowth.

Drill Deformities

Another cause of the 'wandering hole' phenomenon, a bent drill will not spin strait so the tip and/or top of the drill will wobble about this makes it much harder to control the drill as it spins and can lead to the burn in the hearth board to wander and become bigger than the tip of the drill. This can be rectified by a bit of whittling to straighten the drill. The drill doesn't have to be perfectly symmetrical slightly fatter in the middle or a gradual taper all the way along is fine but a bend or kink will make things more difficult.

Flat spots or sharp angles on the drill can also create a problem for example; the string will wear out faster over the sharper angles it may also 'bump' around the drill rather than run smoothly making it harder to hold steady. The rough movement of the drill will require more force and energy to spin it causing you to tire out quicker and as you apply more force, as with the drill that was too wide the tip of the drill will be pulled off course making it more likely to cause a 'wandering hole' and slip out of the hearth.

If the drill is too short either because it started off short or because it has worn away through constant use it will become harder and harder to control. The best position to control the bow drill and apply maximum pressure is to lock the wrist of the arm holding the bearing block against your shin and hold it there this will mean that you can hold the drill perfectly steady. If the drill is so short (less than four inches) that you are having to move your hand lower to a position where you can't rest your wrist against you shin you will find it harder to control. Also a shorter drill gives you less margin for error if the bow string should start to rise or fall along the length of the drill. If you are particularly happy with the drill, maybe one that you have used a lot successfully but is getting too short, or you can only find a small piece of suitable wood for a drill you can fit the short section into the tip of a longer strait section of stick which will act as the shaft of the drill as in the picture bellow;

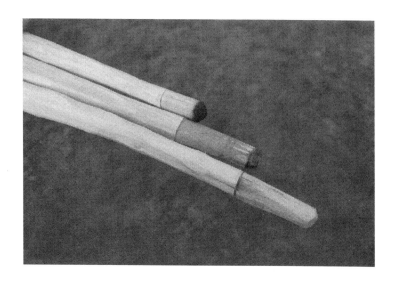

Some finished two piece drills, from top to bottom; holly
shaft with birch tip, dogwood shaft with elder tip, dogwood
shaft with clematis tip.

Two Piece Drill Tutorial;

First take your chosen drill
and dowel the end of it that
will attach to the shaft (as
shown to the left). Next drill
into the tip of the drill shaft to
produce a depression that you
can fit the dowelled end of
the drill tip into. Make sure

that this dowel is at least a couple of centimetres long. If you are using modern glue all you need to do now is fill the hole with glue, force the two sections together and leave it to dry. If you are planning to use more primitive methods take the drill shaft and split the section you have drilled out carefully into four sections now force the drill tip into the shaft, without letting the shaft split all the way, glue in place with pine pitch glue or hoof glue and then bind it with something suitably strong, I would recommend some wet rawhide which will shrink as it dries and hold the drill in place tightly.

The Drill Gets Shiny

Sometimes, as a result of friction, the drill can become polished and shiny rather than charring and producing heat. The shiny polished surface produces much less friction and won't produce an ember. The picture below shows an ivy drill and hearth which has become polished, to rectify this a new point needs to be carved onto the drill to remove the polished wood.

This may be a problem with the material you have selected, perhaps you have selected a very hard wood such as oak which will produce very little friction and polish easily, but this is not always the case. If you are sure you have a good wood for bow drill fire lighting (such as the ivy pictured on the last page) but it is still polishing up and becoming shiny you need to carve off the polished point and begin drilling again. You could also try dropping a few grains of sand into the depression in the hearth to increase friction.

'Smoking Hand'

This is what I call it when you are producing as much or more smoke from the contact between the bearing block and the drill as between the hearth and the drill. This could be for a number of reasons; perhaps the bearing block you are using is made of very dry wood and is creating a lot of friction against the top portion of the drill? Whatever the reason this increased friction now at two ends instead of just one will make the drill harder to spin, it will also mean that much of the energy you are putting into the task is going to the wrong place and ultimately any heat being produced between the drill and bearing block is not helping to create an ember.

To combat the 'smoking hand' try the following;

- Make sure your bearing block is of hard, preferably green wood to reduce friction and provide a degree of lubrication.
- Make sure the depression in the bearing block does not get too deep, if it does the sides of the drill will start to connect with it and produce unwanted friction. If it does

start to get quite deep either take a slice off the bottom of the bearing block or make a new one.

- Make sure the top of the drill does not fit too snugly into the bearing block as this will create more friction. The tip of the drill in the picture  above reaches about half a centimetre into the bearing block depression in the bearing block and contacts the side of the depression all the way around, this causes massive friction and produces the 'smoking hand'

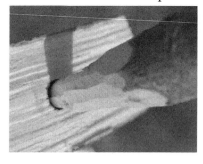 effect. The picture to the left shows the same drill after sharpening reducing the size of the point and the same bearing block after taking a slice off it to reduce the depth of the depression. This reduces the friction produced at this contact point and allows it to spin faster and easier.

- Try carving a depression and setting a limpet shell in it, the inside of the shell is always very smooth, will minimise friction and won't wear out. You won't be able to hold the shell in your bare hand as it will heat up very fast but if you can't set the shell into a wooden bearing block you could always stack two on top of each other.

- Maintain a good sharp point on the top of the drill that will produce minimal friction with the bearing block.

- Try lubricating the point of contact between drill and bearing block, green leaves or a slug will do the job admirably, some of the students that took part in this project even used chainsaw chain oil.

The Hearth Board Is Too Thick

If the hearth board is very thick you may find that as you drill further into it the sides of the drill start to rub against the inside of the depression you have created. Although this would potentially increase the friction between the hearth and drill it does make it very hard to drill. You can beat this in two ways; either make a thinner hearth board or carve away the sides of the drill to produce a thinner point to the drill which won't contact the sides of the depression you have formed. You will also find that the contact point between drill and hearth heats up faster the thinner the hearth is.

This picture shows a hearth that has been drilled all the way through to the ground and which will be of now further use. You can see that the sides of the depression are charred showing where the drill has contacted.

The Bow Is Bending When I Try To Drill

This will happen if you select a bow which is not rigid enough. The bow should be inflexible; you are using it to turn the drill not fire an arrow. If the bow is bendy you will find that if the string is tight enough when you start to drill instead of the drill turning the friction between string and drill will be too much for the bow to overcome and it will just bend instead. To make sure you have a suitable bow aim to find something that is about as long as your arm from arm pit to wrist. This should be from green wood as dead wood is often too weak to stand the rigours of drilling. Select woods that are fairly stiff without being too thick or heavy; sycamore, oak, hawthorn and field maple are all good examples but there is no need to be picky about this the material is not as crucial as with the hearth and drill. Some woods which may not be suitable include willow and poplar which are very flexible and are unlikely to be rigid enough for a successful bow.

Method and Technique

More Pressure

There is a need to gradually apply more pressure as you drill, if you start off with too much pressure you won't be able to turn the drill so start gently and once you have achieved a rhythm with the bow you can increase the pressure. However as it is easier to spin the drill when less pressure is applied it is tempting just to keep drilling without applying the final pressure that is necessary as it feels like you are making progress if you are drilling fast and producing some smoke, however you may find that it takes a very long time to produce an ember or rather than producing a smouldering black ember you instead produce brown dust which is not hot enough to combust.

To help you apply more pressure you could work as a team; make a very long bearing block which two people can hold onto, one at each end. You could combine this with doubling up on the bow as well as in the picture below.

In this picture I am using a normal size bow, drill and hearth but a much larger bearing block made from dogwood. I am holding one end of it locked against my shin and the student is holding the other end, in this way we were able to apply much more pressure and speed and produced an ember very quickly.

Another option is to build a jig which will provide the downward pressure you need without you needing to exert yourself too much or even stabilise the top of the drill yourself. As shown in the picture to the left this setup consists of a heavy log which rests on the ground at one end and on the other has a depression identical to the depression in a bearing block. This end is leant on the top of the drill and is held in place with two uprights sticks knocked firmly into the ground. These sticks can be

squeezed together with the hand that would normally hold the bearing block to stop the log rolling as the drill spins. Trap the hearth in place with your foot and then use the bow in your other hand as normal. As long as the log is heavy enough you now have a setup which allows you to drill without having to manually put pressure on the drill.

I Can't Hold The Drill Steady

Possibly the single most important aspect of successfully lighting a fire with a bow drill is finding a comfortable, effective position to work in. Not only does that position need to be comfortable for you to work in but you need to make sure that you can use one foot to hold the hearth still or it will slide around as you drill. You also need to be able to hold the drill steady, if the drill is not steady and wobbles about you will suffer from issues covered earlier such as 'wandering hole'. The best way I have found to hold the drill steady is shown in the picture below; wrap your arm around your thigh outside of the knee and then

lock your wrist against your shin. This will hold the drill perfectly steady and allow you to lean onto the drill with most of your
weight. As you drill you should also aim to keep the

knuckles of the hand that is operating the bow parallel with the ground at all times. Not only will this stop you skinning your knuckles against the ground but it will also stop the string moving diagonally in relation to the drill. This diagonal movement will cause the string to rise up or drop down the length of the drill and either slip off the top or bottom. To stop this use the ground as your marker, keep your knuckles parallel with it and move your hand smoothly back and forth, don't lose track of where your hand is as you will find that as you gradually increase the speed and pressure of your drilling you will forget about your bow hand and slip back into the habit of sea-sawing up and down. After a bit of practice keeping your drilling steady will become automatic and you'll save yourself a lot of pain and frustration.

Use The Whole Bow

I would normally recommend using as long a bow as you can handle (the length of your arm from armpit to wrist is a good guide) as this means that you get more revolutions of the drill for each stroke of the bow. This makes your technique more efficient and means you need less energy to produce an ember. What you need to make sure is that you are using the whole length of the bow string; lots of short bow strokes will tire you out faster than fewer slower full length strokes and will result in fewer revolutions of the bow, shorter strokes will also mean more time is spent pausing between the forward and backward strokes; allowing the contact point between hearth and drill to cool down and also making the drilling more jerky and therefore harder to control and hold steady.

The Drill Keeps Slipping Off The Hearth

A few of the potential reasons for this have been addressed in the material section but technique plays a part as well. If you rock back and forth as you drill rather than staying steady you will find that you will tilt the hearth board back and forth slightly and also even though you may be holding the drill steady in relation to your body if you are moving it will be too, this rocking can sometimes cause the tip of the drill to slip off the hearth. To make sure you stay steady as you drill check that you are drilling on the flattest piece of ground available, it's also worth whittling the bottom of the hearth as flat as possible to make sure it can't move around.

Managing Your Ember and Lighting a Fire

I Have Made An Ember I Think?

A pile of black dust however much smoke was being made while you were drilling is not necessarily automatically a sign that you have created an ember. It needs to be smoking on its own even when you stop drilling. There is no rush to get it immediately into the tinder bundle; in fact I would suggest that you wait a moment until the ember is well established and glowing.

The picture above shows an unsuccessful ember showing no sign of smoke or a glowing centre.

The process of lighting a fire from a successful ember; here

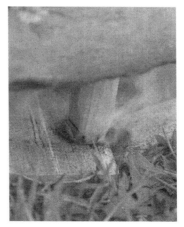

plenty of smoke is being produced with an elm drill on an elm hearth, continue to drill for a few (up to 20) strokes of the bow. Stop drilling and carefully lift the drill away from the hearth without disturbing the ember. The picture below shows the ember after the hearth was removed, you can see the small amount of smoke

being produced. As you fan the ember with your hand or blow it gently it will continue to smoke and before long you will see it begin to glow in the centre, at this stage you need to introduce it to a prepared tinder bundle.

The Ember Falls Apart When I Put It In The Tinder Bundle

You need to make sure your tinder bundle is packed quite tight. Even a well-established ember like the one in the picture to the left is very fragile and will fall apart and drop through the gaps in the tinder bundle if it is not tight and fine enough. Suitable tinder's for taking an ember produced by friction are described here in the same way as suitable woods on pages 28-32;

Species		Notes
Birch bark	C	An excellent tinder in other respects, birch bark would not be my first choice for friction fire lighting. The bark can be shredded and used but is generally too coarse for use with the

very fine embers that you produce by friction. You can add a bit of cat tail down or a cramp ball to this tinder to help if need be.

This combination of birch bark and shaving from a pole lathe would normally be much too coarse for use with embers produced from friction but the addition of a bit of cat tail down or a cramp ball makes it just possible.

Thicker pieces of bark rolled into a tube can also be used, if you stuff a

		tube of bark full of tinder and drop your ember in there you not only avoid burning your fingers but it means you can easily contain your ember and control the amount of air getting to it.
Bracken	**B**	A relatively coarse tinder and will be easier to use if you can add some cat tail down or a cramp ball, or a finer tinder to the heart of the bundle.
Cat tail down	**A**	As a component of your tinder bundle this is fantastic but you will need **more than just cat tail.** It will extend the life of your ember and provide a good hot centre to your tinder bundle but it will not produce the flame you want, you can add a small bit to the centre of any tinder bundle but it really comes into its own when you only have coarse tinder and need to extend the life and size of your ember to produce a flame.

Cedar bark	A	Great tinder if you can find it, it needs to be buffed vigorously to produce a fine nest of tinder but it really is fantastic.
Cramp Ball	A	Another tinder which won't produce a flame for you but which will extend your small friction ember and help the fire lighting process. 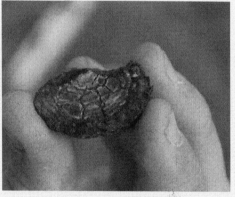 This little fungus will glow like a piece of charcoal and they are worth their weight in gold if you are short of really fine dry tinder. Remember thought that they must be dry themselves, if you knock them off a tree still living they will actually be

		very wet inside, so collect them in advance and break them in half to dry out.
Dry Grass	B	This requires a bit of careful selection and preparation, the stems of grasses will be very poor tinder, it is the leafy matter that you need, this can be collected quite quickly by running your fingers through clumps of dead grass this should pull away the leaves and leave the stalks standing so you don't have to spend too long picking out the stems before you can use the tinder. Late summer is the best time to find dry grass in plentiful supply.
Honeysuckle bark	A	This can be quite plentiful and strips easily of the vines in long fine shreds; it can be buffed further by rubbing it together vigorously and is one of my favourite tinder's.
Straw	C	Much the same as bracken, relatively coarse tinder and without the benefit

	of the leafy fronds of bracken but again with the addition of finer tinder at the heart of a bundle of straw it can work very well.

The Ember Grows At First But Then Goes Out

There could be a number of reasons for this, first just because you start blowing gently doesn't mean you continue blowing gently the whole time, as the ember grows blow harder. As the ember grows it needs more air, if you don't blow hard enough you won't be providing this air.

The second reason might be that your whole tinder bundle is not dry, the ember may have taken in the driest part of the bundle but if there is a damp spot in there it won't be able to ignite that tinder and may well go out. You need to make sure that your **whole** tinder bundle is as dry as possible.

I Get Smoke In My Eyes

This often happens when trying to blow an ember into life, you obviously need to hold it close to your face to blow it but it's very easy to end up as a coughing, spluttering mess with tears streaming down your face as you try to produce a flame. There is a simple solution to this; once you have blown into the tinder bundle and need to take a breath move the bundle away from your face so you have space to breathe without inhaling a load of smoke, when you are ready to blow again move the bundle back up to your face. The rush of air as you move the bundle will also help feed the ember, just remember that just as you start to blow on the ember gently you need to move the bundle gently at first and then as the ember grows you can move it faster. But try not to drop it or move it so fast that it falls apart.

If there is a good strong breeze you can try holding the tinder bundle in the air and just let the wind do the job.

I Made Fire!! Now what?

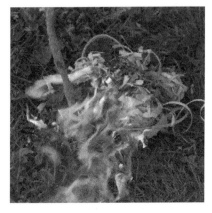 Remember that even if you have a flame you don't have a fire yet, you need to prepare everything well in advance. **All** your kindling and medium sized fuel needs to be ready along with extra tinder if you should need it. Once you have a flame your tinder bundle may not last long so get it to your kindling as soon as possible. You may need to be quite hands on with it slowly adding the finest pieces of kindling a piece at a time at first to avoid demolishing the tinder bundle. Once it is going you can safely start to add handfuls of fine kindling and then larger pieces just as you would normally.

Activities for teaching the bow drill

Learning Logs;

There may be a number of reasons for their ineffectiveness. One may be, and I possibly should have realized this in advance, that this group of students prefers practical activities to theory based teaching and writing. This would make them 'kinesthetic' learners in the language of learning styles, although there is no evidence to confirm that assigning 'learning styles' to students based on their completion of a test such as a VARK questionnaire is reliable (Pashler, et al., 2008) nor that matching delivery to those preferences is automatically beneficial (Coffield, et al., 2004). However I am convinced of the usefulness of learning logs in some form as they have been so useful to me, perhaps if I had allowed the students to come up with their own method for reflecting on their performance some would have chosen a similar method without my intervention while others would have responded better to other methods.

Peer Teaching

Those students who had been successful early in the project were able to provide direction and help to others who struggled or had missed sessions, not only did it help the student being taught but it meant that the 'teaching' students could watch someone else's technique and approach and potential apply what they learned about their friends successes and mistakes. Also the process of teaching in itself meant that they continued to practice and hone their own technique perhaps past the point that they would have if they had just been practicing on their own.

Recording comments

This proved particularly effective and helped me measure the student's grasp of the task even when they did not use their learning logs. I triggered this activity by writing down a few comments I had heard students make while they worked on their fire lighting and encouraging them to write down ideas they had or conclusions they had come to. At the end of the session they each identified what they had said and even looked at what other people had said to inform their plan of action for the next session, so they benefitted from other experience as well. The picture bellow shows a whiteboard full of comments after one session;

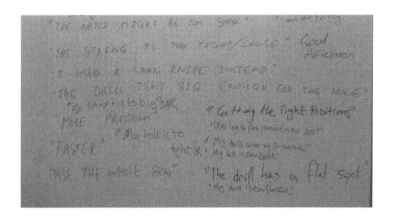

'Speed dating'

I use this activity a lot in other sessions, normally in a slightly different format where students will be assigned a topic to learn or one which I know they have a lot of experience of and over the course of a few minutes depending on time and number of students they will have to speak to each of their peers and glean as much information about each topic as they can. I modified this exercise for this specific setting and asked students to explain as much of the following as possible to each of their peers in the 'speed date format';

- What types of wood did you try today?
- Demonstrate your stance for bow drill fire lighting
- Did your bow/hearth/bearing block combo make any funny noises?
- Did you produce 'char dust'?
- Did you produce smoke?
- What did you do to progress from just producing dust and smoke to produce an ember?

Socratic questioning

As I gave feedback to students to help direct their reflections I found myself filling a coaching role, as I often do as a teacher. Coaching is an important part of instructing skills but the coaching students received from me often comes in the form of Socratic questioning (named after Socrates, and based on his method of teaching with questions) to draw from them information or understanding they already had. It is my experience that often perhaps due to a lack of confidence or to avoid being seen as a swot or teacher's pet students are sometimes reluctant to volunteer information. When stretched by this form of questioning, on an individual basis if necessary, they often demonstrate a much greater understanding than they might do if asked simple direct questions.

Team Activities

Many of these activities help students not just give feedback and advice to each other but also lead them to collaborate. During the project several students formed teams to work on fire lighting in two's or even threes to make the task easier. Because of their involvement with the task and each other the students were able to give very valuable feedback to each other. This feedback also gave learners another opinion to base their own reflection and personal reviews on which might influence how they progress to change and develop their practice and explore and imagine alternative ways of going about the task next time. Additionally the fact that students were able to give each other valuable feedback and critically evaluate not only their own performance but the performance of others in their groups demonstrated a deeper understanding of the task and its method. The team bow drill method pictured earlier is a perfect way to promote team work as well as an effective way of helping those who may not have the physical ability to work on their own.

Conclusion

The interesting thing about the advice presented here is that I discovered it for myself through trial and error, as did my students who were involved with this project. Of course you **could** be taught this by an instructor or teacher but even though they may know all these things and more, having done it themselves hundreds if not thousands of times they are trying to help you succeed in a limited amount of time which may mean you won't be given the opportunity to fail enough times to learn all these things for yourself. While they may have shown you the correct way to do it and you may be able to light a fire using that exact method and the those materials you prepared or were given during that instruction what happens when you encounter a new problem or can't find the type of wood you used the first time? I'm not saying that being taught bushcraft by an instructor is bad but I strongly believe that there needs to be an element of self-directed learning in whatever you do as it gives you ownership of what you have learned and indeed helps you remember and apply what you have learned.

Regarding my stated aim for this project; to promote deeper learning. The fact that the students began to recognise what they needed to change about their technique and make those changes shows that they have developed more than an unconscious competence of the task. They have also been able to demonstrate that they can apply a wider knowledge of bushcraft and countryside management to the task, particularly in relation to the selection of materials. Their experience of countryside management means that the students already have a deeper understanding of certain aspects of the task than many people who might only practice bushcraft as a recreational activity. They should already know how to identify tree and shrub species which might provide the necessary materials and in turn practicing bushcraft might help develop their identification skills further. Also as they try different materials, by trial and error and by reflecting on the relative effectiveness of each different hearth, drill and bearing block they might conclude that, for example; of clematis, sycamore and hazel, clematis is the easiest to produce an ember with, this would be a valuable observation but a deeper understanding would help them go further and say that not only does clematis produce an ember best but it matches the description of the kind of wood we should be using, based on that description and their new knowledge of the necessary properties of the material when clematis is unavailable they can find an alternative that demonstrates some similar characteristics and use that successfully.

References

Coffield, F., Moseley, D., Hall, E. & Ecclestone, K., 2004. *Learning Stykes and Pedagogy in Post-16 Learning; A sustematic and critical review* , Trowbridge: Learning and Skills Research Centre

Houghton, W., 2004. *Engineering Subject Centre Guide: Learning and Teaching Theory for Engineering Academics.* Loughborough: HEA Engineering Subject Centre .

Jensen, V., 1987. 'Writing in college physics'. In: T. Fulwiler, ed. *The Journal Book.* Portsmouth NH: Heinemann.

Laurillard , D., 1993. *Rethinking University Teaching.* London: Routledge .

Moon , J., 2006. *Learning journals : a handbook for reflective practice and professional development.* 2nd ed. Abingdon: Routledge .

Pashler, H., McDaniel, M., Rohrer, D. & Bjork, R., 2008. Learning Styles; Concepts and Evidence. *Psychological Science in the Public Interest* , 9(3), pp. 105-119.

Petty, G., 2004. *Teaching Today.* 3rd ed. Cheltenham: Nelson Thornes Ltd.

Piolat, A., Olive, T. & Kellogg, R., 2005. Cognitive Effort During Note Taking. *Aplied Cognitive Psychology,* Volume 19, pp. 291-312.

Schon, D., 1987. *Educating the Reflective Practitioner; Toward a New Design for Teaching and Learning in the Professions.* San Francisco: Jossey-Bass.

BushcraftEducation

BushcraftEducation is a blog which I write and manage with the aim of sharing ideas of how to use what has become known as 'bushcraft' in educational settings. I would probably attribute the term bushcraft to Ray Mears or Mors_Kochanski, prior to their books on the topic the skills now known as bushcraft would have been called 'survival skills' and were often based closely on military survival training.

Bushcraft seems to me to be based more on native and primitive skills and the idea that you can use your skills to live in the woods and wild places rather than merely survive them. Also whereas learning survival skills might have been seen as an emergency preparedness measure bushcraft is a hobby or leisure time activity which doesn't need to be so regimented or extreme.

I have become convinced by my experiences of teaching bushcraft, forest schools, environmental education and countryside and wildlife management that bushcraft can, and indeed **should** be used as a tool in all forms of teaching. I have seen my own children's enthusiasm and understanding of nature grow at a young age and their skills develop as a result of taking part in Bushcraft activities. I have seen students of all ages benefit from the growing experiences provided by being outdoors, I've heard comments such as; **"all students were totally engaged, even those that sometimes find it difficult"** and **"Learners found it easier to engage with sessions"** from staff and learning support assistants who accompanied a group of special needs students I taught for several session where I integrated bushcraft to support their 'land-based studies' curriculum.

I've also seen students who engaged with bushcraft sessions on plant identification drastically outperform those who did not take part in any buschraft tuition in a plant identification test. In my observations of the students I heard some of them referring to their bushcraft experiences; **"I remember eating that it tasted awful"** and **"that's the one we used to make friction fire kits"** this additional experience which may have been more engaging than the guide books, dichotomous keys and classrooms where the other group had learned may have been the difference between average test scores of 56% for the group not taking part in bushcraft and 81% for the group which did

In this blog I share my thoughts and ideas for using bushcraft as a tool in education and also touch on closely related subjects such as primitive skills, fieldsports, game and wildlife management, green woodwork, wildfood etc.. which can all be enfolded under the umbrella term of bushcraft and which all need to be represented and used in mainstream education as well as by specialist providers to give the young people of this day and age a better chance to engage with nature and the environment and make up their own minds about what it is and what their place in it should be.

Please visit;

www.bushcrafteducation.blogspot.co.uk

find the Bushcraft Education Facebook page and follow me on twitter **@GdaGuy** for regular updates

Thanks

Geoff

30231048R00055

Printed in Great Britain
by Amazon